Hamlyn Gardening Guide

SHRUBS AND CLIMBING PLANTS

Alan Toogood

HAMLYN

ACKNOWLEDGEMENTS
Cover photograph by The Harry Smith Horticultural
Photographic Collection.
Colour photographs
Allen Paterson, p. 10; Photos Horticultural, p. 12, 60; The
Harry Smith Horticultural Photographic Collection, 5, 8.
All other photographs by Rob Herwig.

Published in 1986 by
Hamlyn Publishing,
Bridge House, London Road,
Twickenham, Middlesex, England

ISBN 0 600 30720 4

Filmset in 9½pt on 11½pt Palatino
by Page Bros (Norwich) Ltd, England

Printed and bound in Italy

CONTENTS

INTRODUCTION

*T*o give a garden an established appearance you will need to plant some permanent subjects, as opposed to temporary plants like annuals and spring and summer bedding plants. Shrubs and climbers are ideal for this purpose, together with conifers, particularly dwarf kinds.

But what are shrubs? They are woody plants – that is, they have a permanent 'framework' of several or many woody stems. They may be deciduous (drop their leaves in autumn), or evergreen (retain their foliage all the year round). Many are grown for their flowers, which may be produced in any one of the four seasons, some for their coloured foliage, others for coloured stems or berries.

Shrubs come in all sizes, from prostrate ground-hugging kinds, through medium-sized kinds, around 1.2 to 1.8 m (4 to 6 ft) in height, to large specimens which may reach 3.6 m (12 ft) or more. So there is something for every size of garden.

Generally, climbers are even taller, although some attain only 1.8 to 2.4 m (6 to 8 ft) in height. Again they are woody-stemmed, permanent plants, but due to their height and thinnish stems need some means of support – walls, fences or trellis. Climbers may also be deciduous or evergreen, flower during any one of the four seasons, or provide attractive berries. Some climbers will support themselves by means of their twisting or twining stems; tendrils which grip any convenient object; aerial roots or even by tiny sucker pads which 'stick' to flat walls and fences.

Conifers are essentially shrubs, and most are evergreen. Again they can vary from prostrate kinds to large or giant specimens. Popular with today's small-garden owners are the dwarf conifers, of which there are many to choose from. Conifers differ from other shrubs in that they produce their seeds in 'cones' instead of in normal seed capsules, pods and berries.

A collection of shrubs, climbers and conifers will not only provide a

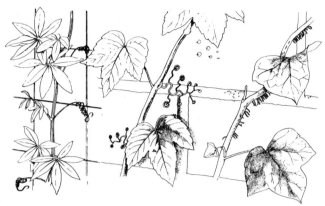

Some climbers support themselves by means of tendrils (clematis), sucker pads (Boston ivy) or aerial roots (ivy)

permanent living 'framework' for a garden, it will ensure, if carefully chosen, colour and interest all the year round.

Cultivation

Buying plants

There are various places to buy shrubs, climbers and conifers. For instance, you can buy mail-order from one of the specialist shrub growers, who all produce descriptive catalogues. They offer the widest possible range of varieties. Plants are sent out at the correct planting time. Depending on subject, the plant may be in a pot or it may be bare-rooted (lifted from the open ground) with the roots wrapped to prevent drying out.

Many people will, however, buy from a local garden centre where the plants are supplied in either rigid pots or in flexible polythene pots (or 'bags'). There is a more limited selection of varieties at garden centres, which tend to stock only the most popular kinds.

However, the beauty of buying plants in pots is that they can be planted at any time of year, provided the ground is not too wet or frozen. You can choose plants which are in flower and plant for immediate effect. You can inspect plants before buying to ensure they are of good quality.

Many garden centres arrange displays of shrubs for each month of the year to show customers what is in season.

Do inspect garden-centre plants closely before you buy to make sure the quality is good. Watch for the following points. The plant should be well-established in its pot, with perhaps a few small roots showing through the bottom. The plant should not be loose in the pot and the compost should be moist and free from weeds. Climbers should be tied in to a cane. Leaves should look healthy, not yellowing or have brown spots, patches or leaf edges. Shrubs should be well-branched to the base and conifers should have foliage right to the base. Shrubs and conifers should be of a good shape – not lop-sided, for instance.

If you are buying at flowering time the plant should have plenty of flower buds, with a few blooms open; and each plant should be labelled with its name.

All year round interest

Spring can be welcomed by many flowering shrubs, including berberis, camellias, chaenomeles, cytisus, forsythia, kerria, ribes, syringa (lilac) and wisteria. Rhododendrons will also be in flower, and they extend into summer, when the display is continued with philadelphus (mock orange), escallonias, weigelas, heathers, clematis and buddleias. Autumn may be heralded by colourful berries of berberis, cotoneasters, euonymus and pyracantha; and by the brilliant leaf tints of acers, rhus and vitis.

No garden should 'die' in winter, for there are many flowering shrubs to choose from, like *Cornus mas*, hamamelis (witch hazels), mahonias, *Erica herbacea, E.* × *darleyensis* and *Jasminum nudiflorum*. Shrubs with coloured stems come into their own, like *Cornus alba*, as do the evergreens such as *Elaeagnus pungens* 'Maculata' and, of course, the dwarf conifers with foliage in gold, 'blue', grey or various shades of green.

Where to grow

Shrubs can be grown in various parts of the garden. For instance, you may prefer to have a border or bed devoted purely to shrubs – very labour saving. As has been indicated already, there will be no fear of colourless periods if you choose something for every month of the year.

Many people will, however, prefer to have mixed beds or borders, including many kinds of plants. The 'framework' of a mixed border, though, can consist of shrubs. Around and between these can be planted herbaceous perennials, bulbs, annuals, spring and summer bedding plants.

Some shrubs – those with a particularly distinctive habit of growth – can be grown in isolation as specimen plants, which act as focal points to lead the eye to various parts of a garden. For instance, you may want a shrub or two in the lawn, or perhaps at the end of a path.

Suitably distinctive shrubs include *Buddleia alternifolia, Cornus florida* 'Rubra' and *C. kousa, Corylus avellana* 'Contorta', ilex varieties, *Parrotia persica, Rhus typhina* 'Laciniata', and *Yucca flaccida*.

Conifers can be used in the same way, like chamaecyparis, juniperus and taxus. A bed of mixed dwarf conifers also looks good, if you choose various shapes and colours. A bed of dwarf conifers and heathers is even more impressive as there are heathers available for flowering throughout the four seasons. Both schemes are extremely labour-saving as conifers and heathers need very little attention.

Climbers can be used wherever there is vertical space – they can be grown up walls, fences and free-standing trellis screens. They can

Clematis, honeysuckle and climbing roses intermingle against a stone wall

be trained up large trees and even over large shrubs. For the latter, clematis cultivars can be particularly recommended. Grow climbers, too, over arches and pergolas, over the garage or shed, or even erect tall wooden posts (fencing posts are ideal) for them in the shrub or mixed border. Some climbers can even be used as ground cover, particularly on steep banks, including clematis, hedera (ivy), lonicera (honeysuckle), parthenocissus and vitis.

When planting shrubs to form the framework of a bed, border or garden, one generally aims to avoid too many evergreens, as they can result in a 'heavy' sombre effect reminiscent of Victorian 'shrubberies'. Aim for a balance of one-third evergreens and two-thirds deciduous shrubs, and spread out evergreens well – in other words, mix them with the deciduous kinds.

Correct conditions

Shrubs, conifers and climbers must be chosen with regard to the conditions in your garden – the aspect and soil.

For instance, there are many plants which need a sunny position, and which would not grow or flower well in shade. At the other extreme there are plenty of subjects for shady or partially shady areas. See the A to Z section of the book for examples.

Some plants are tolerant of very exposed positions, surviving cold winds, while others are not so tough and must have a sheltered aspect.

Shrubs must also be suited to your particular soil. For instance, there are some which must have acid or lime-free conditions, such as the rhododendrons and camellias. There are others, and plenty of them, which can be grown in chalky or limy soils.

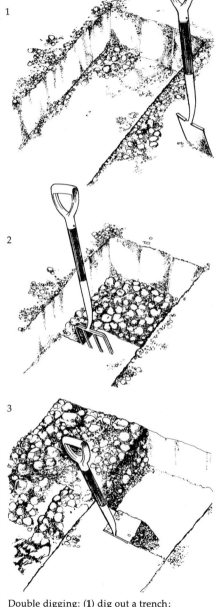

Double digging: (1) dig out a trench; (2) break up the bottom soil; (3) fill in with soil from the adjacent strip incorporating bulky organic material as you go

There are several, too, which will thrive in wet soils. Again I would refer you to the A to Z section of the book.

Preparing the soil
As shrubs, climbers and conifers will remain where they are planted for many years, it is important to prepare the soil thoroughly before planting to ensure good growth in subsequent years.

The first priority is to eradicate perennial weeds, like ground elder, bindweed and couch grass, as these are more difficult to control once shrubs are planted.

Perennial weeds can be sprayed with weedkiller containing glyphosate, and when they are dead digging can commence. Deep digging (known as double digging), to a depth of two spade blades, is recommended in order to break up the lower soil, to ensure surplus water drains away and deep rooting of the shrubs can take place.

While digging add bulky organic matter to each trench – about a quarter of a barrowload to each 1.2-m (4-ft) length of trench. Use garden compost, well-rotted manure, mushroom compost, spent hops or, more expensive, peat or shredded bark. If you are growing mainly rhododendrons, camellias and other lime-hating plants, then peat or bark would be the best soil additives. If possible allow the ground to settle for a couple of months before planting.

Before buying shrubs it would be advisable to test the soil for acidity

Rhododendrons and azaleas or other calcifuges can be grown in a tub of ericaceous compost if your soil is too alkaline

or alkalinity, to find out whether or not it contains lime or chalk. If it does you will not be able to grow lime-hating plants. So buy one of the inexpensive soil-testing kits, and use according to the instructions supplied. If the soil has a pH of 6.5 or below it is acid, and you will be able to grow rhododendrons, azaleas and camellias. If it is above pH 7 it is alkaline. Most shrubs can be grown in acid conditions – even the chalk loving plants do not necessarily need alkaline soil.

If you have very badly drained soil, such as heavy clay, it is recommended that you add coarse sand or grit while digging, in addition to bulky organic matter. These materials will keep the soil open and so improve drainage.

Planting
As I have already indicated, shrubs in containers can be planted at any time of year, provided the ground

is not very wet or frozen, as the rootball is not disturbed. However, I should add that I prefer, whenever possible, to plant evergreens (including conifers) in April or May, or in September/ October, as the plants get established very much quicker at these times of the year; because the soil is warming up in spring and is still warm in the autumn. If you buy evergreens lifted from the open ground, with their roots enclosed in a ball of soil wrapped with hessian, netting or polythene, then you should certainly only plant in spring or autumn.

Deciduous shrubs and climbers which have been lifted from the open ground are planted when they are dormant – between November and March.

Pot- or container-grown subjects are the easiest to plant. First water them thoroughly to make sure the compost is moist. Carefully remove the pot to avoid root disturbance. If the plant is in a flexible polythene bag, slit this down one side and underneath and carefully peel it off.

Take out a hole slightly wider than the diameter of the rootball and of such a depth that after planting the top of the rootball is about 1 cm (½ in) below the surrounding soil level. Set the plant centrally in the hole and return fine soil around it, firming well with your heels as you proceed.

Evergreens with a rootball (lifted from the open ground) are planted in the same way, after carefully removing the wrapping material.

With bare-rooted deciduous shrubs you must take out a large enough hole to ensure the roots can be spread out to their full extent. The shrub should be planted to the same depth – indicated by a soil mark at the base of the stems. Fine soil should first be worked well between the roots, by returning a few spadesful over the roots and then gently shaking the plant up and down. Then add more soil, firming as you go with your heels.

If you feel that your soil is very poor (such as light and sandy, chalky, gravelly, or even heavy clay) consider using a proprietary planting mixture. This is basically peat with fertilisers added. It is mixed into the soil in the bottom of the planting hole and also into the soil which is to be returned around the plant. This gets shrubs, climbers and conifers off to a really good start.

Regarding planting distances you must allow each shrub sufficient space to spread to its full extent. Sizes are given in the A to Z section of the book. The shrubs will look too widely spaced to start with, but these spaces can be filled temporarily with, for example, herbaceous perennials, bulbs, annuals or spring and summer bedding.

Wherever possible you will create a better effect if you plant

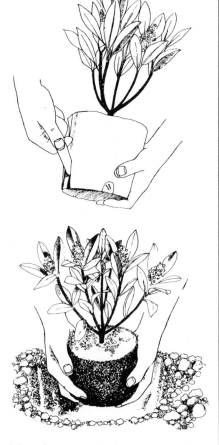

When planting a container-grown shrub, always remember to remove the polythene sleeve before planting

shrubs in groups of one variety (say three plants in each group) instead of single specimens. Although, of course, this is not possible with large or even medium-sized shrubs in small gardens. However, you should certainly try to use this method for very small shrubs, including such subjects as heathers, potentillas, ceratostigma, skimmia, vincas and the like.

Aftercare
Don't just plant and forget! If plants are to establish well they need looking after.

Evergreens (including conifers) should be prevented from losing too much moisture through their leaves after planting. Either spray them, according to directions on the can with a proprietary anti-transpirant aerosol spray or daily with plain water (unless the weather is wet) for a period of six weeks after planting.

Never allow the soil to dry out around newly-planted subjects, so water heavily if the weather is dry. This generally applies only to spring, summer or autumn planting.

To prevent the soil drying out rapidly, and to suppress the growth of weeds, shrubs can with advantage be permanently mulched with organic matter, such as garden compost or well-rotted farmyard manure, mushroom compost, spent hops; or with peat or shredded bark for rhododendrons, azaleas, camellias and other lime-haters. Mulching involves placing a 5- to

Climbers *Actinidia kolomikta* and *Hedera helix* display an interesting contrast in leaf shape and texture

7.5-cm (2- to 3-in) deep layer of one of these materials over the soil surface around the plants, but not right up to the stems. Top up a mulch annually in spring as necessary.

All shrubs, climbers and conifers benefit from feeding. In the spring each year lightly hoe into the soil surface a dressing of general-purpose fertiliser.

Climbers planted against walls and fences will need some means of support, unless they are self supporting. Initially they can be guided to the wall by tying them in to a bamboo cane angled towards the wall.

Horizontal galvanised wires

Use vine eyes to ensure horizontal training wires are kept taut

spaced 30 to 45 cm (12 to 18 in) apart make ideal supports – the stems can be tied to them. The wires can be fixed with 'vine' eyes – there are types suitable for both masonry and fences. Alternatively put up some trellis panels, fixing them with suitable brackets 2.5 to 5 cm (1 to 2 in) away from the wall.

Pruning

Certain shrubs and climbers need regular pruning to encourage flower production, to ensure the plants remain vigorous, and to keep them shapely. Many, however, need no pruning, except for the removal of dead wood as necessary.

Prune immediately after flowering deciduous shrubs which flower in spring or early summer on growths produced in the previous year. Cut back the stems that have flowered to young shoots lower down the stems. Examples of this type of shrub include chaenomeles, cytisus, deutzia, forsythia, *Jasminum nudiflorum*, kerria, philadelphus, spiraeas and weigela.

Deciduous shrubs which flower in the summer and autumn on growths which are formed in the current season should be pruned in early spring, when all stems are cut down to within a few centimetres of the ground. Examples are *Buddleia davidii*, caryopteris, ceanothus, hardy fuchsias, *Hydrangea paniculata* and tamarix.

Coloured-stemmed shrubs are also pruned almost to the ground in early spring. Examples are *Cornus alba* varieties, *C. stolonifera* 'Flaviramea' and *Rubus thibetanus*.

Shrubs which need any dead flowers removed include rhododendrons, azaleas, lilacs, and heathers. The heathers can be trimmed over lightly with shears.

Climbers vary in their pruning requirements and details will be found in the A to Z section of the book.

Pests and diseases

Aphids Greenfly and blackfly can be controlled by spraying with a systemic insecticide containing permethrin and heptenophos.
Caterpillars Many kinds eat foliage. Spray with a systemic insecticide as above.
Honey fungus (*Armillaria*

mellea) A serious disease which can quickly kill shrubs and climbers, by attacking the roots. Dead plants should be dug up and burnt, and the ground sterilised with formaldehyde. Sick-looking plants can be treated with a proprietary armillaria soil drench.
Mildew Many plants can be attacked by this fungal disease, which appears as mealy white patches on leaves and shoot tips. Spray with a systemic fungicide containing propiconazole.

Increasing plants

Stem cuttings
In the spring many shrubs and climbers can be propagated from stem cuttings of soft new side shoots. These should be approximately 7.5 cm (3 in) long, the base of each being cut cleanly across just below a leaf joint or node with a sharp knife. The leaves

Soft cuttings fuchsia are taken in the spring: (1) cut just below a leaf joint; (2) dip base in hormone rooting powder, and (3) insert around the edge of a pot. Cover with a polythene bag until rooted (4)

from the lower half of each cutting are cut off. Dip bases of cuttings in hormone rooting powder, tap off the excess and then insert them up to their lower leaves in pots of cutting compost – equal parts by volume of coarse sand and peat. They will need heat and humidity to root so ideally should be placed in an electrically heated propagating case. Alternatively, enclose each pot in a clear polythene bag (which can be supported above the cuttings with a few short split canes) and stand on a windowsill in a warm room. Rooting generally takes up to six or eight weeks, depending on subject.

Many other shrubs can be prepared from semi-ripe stem cuttings later in the year – from about July to September. They are prepared in the same way as soft cuttings but these cuttings will be hard and woody at the base but still soft and green at the top. Insert in the same way as softwood cuttings, but bear in mind they can be rooted in cooler conditions (although heat will speed rooting), such as a garden frame. Many evergreens and conifers, especially, can be propagated from semi-ripe cuttings.

Hardwood stem cuttings of deciduous shrubs are taken after leaf fall, in the autumn or early winter. Current year's stems are used and they should be fully ripened and hard, or woody. They are cut into sections, each about 15 to 20 cm (6 to 8 in) in length, making the top cut just above a bud and the bottom cut just below

a bud. Use secateurs for preparation as the wood will be hard. Dip in hormone rooting powder and insert the cuttings up to two-thirds of their length, either in a soil bed in a sheltered, well-drained part of the garden, or in a peat and sand bed in a garden frame. The cuttings should be well rooted by the autumn of the following year, when they can be lifted and planted out.

Simple layering
Many shrubs can be propagated by this method, which is much easier, and often more reliable, than taking cuttings. Basically it involves encouraging a young stem to form roots while it is still attached to the parent plant. Once rooted it will develop into a new plant. Layering is best carried out in spring or summer, and is ideal for shrubs which prove difficult to raise from cuttings, like rhododendrons, azaleas, camellias and so on.

Select a young thin stem which can be pulled down to the ground. About 30 cm (12 in) from its tip remove a few leaves to give a bare area of stem. This area must be wounded to encourage it to form roots. The easiest way of wounding is to grip the stem tightly in both hands and give it a sharp twist to break some of the tissues. Alternatively one can cut a 5 cm (2 in) long tongue in the stem, half-way through it. This should be kept open with a small stone or piece of wood.

Now take out a hole in the soil 15 cm (6 in) deep and peg down the wounded part of the stem into it, using a thick piece of wire bent to the shape of a hairpin. Cover with 15 cm (6 in) of soil. The end of the

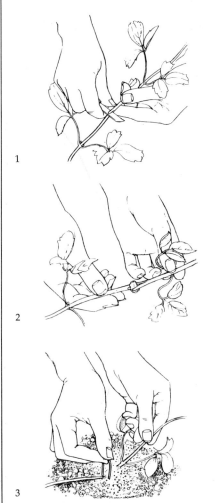

Simple layering: **(1)** partially cut the stem; **(2)** hold the cut open with a stone; **(3)** peg the wounded area down so it is in contact with the soil

stem which is showing above soil level should be gently pulled into an upright position and held with a short bamboo cane and string. Most subjects take at least a year to form a good root system, when they should be lifted and cut away from the parent plant.

Serpentine layering
This is used for climbing plants. A long stem can be encouraged to root in a number of places along its length. Each part of the stem to be pegged down is prepared as described above for simple layering, and the pegging down technique is also the same. Several new plants can be obtained from one stem in this way.

Serpentine layering produces a number of new plants from one stem; a particularly useful method of propagating clematis, honeysuckle and other climbers

Methods of propagation for each subject are given in the A to Z section of the book.

A TO Z
OF SHRUBS
AND
CLIMBING PLANTS

Acer palmatum 'Dissectum' Japanese maple
Habit: deciduous shrub; 3 by 3 m (10 by
10 ft), grown for autumn leaf colour.
Conditions: shelter, partial shade, moist
well-drained soil. **Propagation:** layering in
summer.

Actinidia kolomikta Kolomikta vine
Habit: deciduous climber; height and spread
1.8 to 3.6 m (6 to 12 ft). **Conditions:** best in
acid, rich soil. **Care:** thin out in late winter.
Propagation: semi-ripe cuttings in summer.

Aucuba japonica 'Variegata' Spotted laurel
Habit: evergreen foliage shrub; height and
spread about 1.8 m (6 ft). **Conditions:** any
soil, shade or sun. **Care:** prune back if too
large, in April. **Propagation:** semi-ripe
cuttings in summer.

Berberis × *stenophylla* Barberry
Habit: evergreen spring-flowering shrub;
height and spread about 2.4 m (8 ft).
Conditions: adaptable, any soil (good on
chalk); full sun. **Propagation:** semi-ripe
cuttings in late summer/autumn.

Berberis thunbergii Barberry
Habit: deciduous shrub for autumn berries; height and spread 1.2 by 1.8 m (4 by 6 ft). **Conditions:** best in full sun; takes partial shade. Other comments as for *B.* × *stenophylla.*

Berberis wilsoniae Barberry
Habit: deciduous shrub for flowers and autumn berries, autumn leaf colour; height and spread about 1 m (3 ft). **Conditions:** will take some shade but best in sun. Other comments as for *B.* × *stenophylla.*

Buddleia alternifolia
Habit: deciduous shrub flowering in early summer; height about 3.6 m (12 ft), similar spread. **Conditions:** full sun, well-drained soil, good on chalk. **Propagation:** semi-ripe cuttings in late summer.

Buddleia davidii variety Butterfly bush
Habit: deciduous shrub, flowering late summer, attracting butterflies; height and spread at least 2.4 m (8 ft). **Care:** prune hard back in late winter. **Propagation:** hardwood cuttings in autumn/winter.

Buddleia davidii variety Butterfly bush
Habit, conditions, care and propagation as
previous page. There are many varieties of
Buddleia davidii in a wide range of colours
and most of them have fragrant blooms
which attract various insects.

Calluna vulgaris 'Gold Haze' Ling
Habit: dwarf evergreen heather grown for its
foliage; height about 30 cm (12 in), spread
45 cm (18 in). **Conditions:** full sun, acid soil.
Care: trim lightly after flowering.
Propagation: semi-ripe cuttings

Calluna vulgaris 'H. E. Beale' Ling
Habit: dwarf evergreen heather flowering in
summer; height and spread about 45 cm
(18 in). **Conditions:** full sun, acid soil.
Care: trim lightly after flowering.
Propagation: semi-ripe cuttings, summer.

Camellia japonica
Habit: bushy evergreen shrub flowering in
spring; height and spread 1.8 to 3.6 m (6 to
12 ft) depending on variety. Many varieties
and colours. **Conditions:** acid soil, partial
shade. **Propagation:** layering, spring.

Campsis radicans Trumpet vine
Habit: deciduous climber flowering late
summer; height to 12 m (40 ft).
Conditions: warm, sheltered wall in full sun;
good drainage. **Propagation:** semi-ripe
cuttings in late summer.

Ceanothus 'Gloire de Versailles'
Habit: deciduous shrub, flowering in
summer/autumn; height and spread 2.4 m
(8 ft). **Conditions:** warm sunny wall; good
drainage. **Care:** prune hard in spring.
Propagation: semi-ripe cuttings.

Celastrus orbiculatus Staff vine
Habit: deciduous climber grown for autumn
berries; up to 9 m (30 ft). **Conditions:** any
well-drained soil; shelter from cold winds.
Care: thin out if necessary late winter.
Propagation: semi-ripe cuttings.

Ceratostigma plumbaginoides
Habit: low deciduous shrub; about 30 by
30 cm (12 by 12 in). Flowers late summer.
Conditions: full sun, good drainage.
Care: cut back all old shoots late winter.
Propagation: semi-ripe cuttings.

Cercis siliquastrum Judas tree
Habit: deciduous shrub, flowers in spring; height about 4.5 m (15 ft), similar spread.
Conditions: full sun, shelter, rich soil.
Propagation: best raised from seeds sown in greenhouse in spring.

Chaenomeles speciosa 'Crimson and Gold' Ornamental quince
Habit: deciduous shrub flowering in spring; height and spread up to 1.8 m (6 ft).
Conditions: any well-drained soil, full sun.
Care: thin out old wood after flowering.
Propagation: simple layering.

Chamaecyparis lawsoniana 'Blue Nantais'
Lawson cypress
Habit: a conical evergreen conifer, ideal specimen plant; height to about 9 m (30 ft).
Conditions: open position, well-drained soil.
Care: keep the soil moist. **Propagation:** semi-ripe cuttings in late summer.

Chamaecyparis lawsoniana 'Ellwoodii'
Lawson cypress
Habit: popular, evergreen conifer; height to about 6 m (20 ft). **Conditions:** open position, well-drained soil. **Care:** keep the soil moist.
Propagation: semi-ripe cuttings in late summer.

Chamaecyparis lawsoniana 'Erecta Aurea'
Lawson cypress
Habit: evergreen conifer, one of the many golden-leaved dwarf Lawson cypresses; height 3.6 m (12 ft), spread 2.4 m (6 ft). Full sun needed, otherwise as for *C. l.* 'Ellwoodii'.

Chamaecyparis pisifera 'Boulevard'
Sawara cypress
Habit: popular evergreen conifer; height and spread about 3 m (10 ft). **Conditions:** open position, or slight shade. Good drainage. Suitable for chalky or acid soils. **Propagation:** semi-ripe cuttings.

Chamaecyparis pisifera 'Filifera Aurea'
Sawara cypress
Habit: widely grown evergreen conifer; height and spread about 4.5 m (15 ft) but slow growing. Comments as for *C. p.* 'Boulevard' but must be grown in full sun for the best foliage colour.

Choisya ternata Mexican orange blossom
Habit: evergreen shrub producing scented flowers in spring; height and spread at least 1.8 m (6 ft). **Conditions:** any soil with good drainage; full sun and shelter. **Propagation:** semi-ripe cuttings.

Clematis alpina variety
Habit: climber to about 1.8 m (6 ft), flowering in spring. **Conditions:** stems in sun, roots in shade; ideal for chalky soils. **Care:** prune after flowering only to restrict spread if necessary. **Propagation:** cuttings.

Clematis hybrid 'Ernest Markham'
Habit: deciduous climber to about 3.6 m (12 ft), flowering in summer. **Conditions:** as *alpina.* **Care:** prune in spring – cut back, almost to their bases, all previous year's stems. **Propagation:** as for *alpina.*

Clematis hybrid 'Hagley Hybrid'
Habit: deciduous climber to about 1.8 m (6 ft), flowering in summer. **Conditions:** as *alpina.* **Care:** prune in spring – cut back, almost to their bases, all previous year's stems. **Propagation:** as for *alpina.*

Clematis hybrid 'Nelly Moser'
Habit: deciduous climber to about 3.6 m (12 ft), flowering in summer. **Conditions:** as *alpina.* **Care:** prune in spring; cut back all previous year's stems almost to their bases. **Propagation:** as for *alpina.*

Clematis hybrid 'Vyvyan Pennell'
Habit: deciduous climber to about 3.6 m
(12 ft), flowering in summer. **Conditions:** as
alpina. **Care:** prune in spring – cut back,
almost to their bases, all previous year's
stems. **Propagation:** as for *alpina*.

Clematis × jackmanii
Habit: deciduous climber to about 3.6 m
(12 ft), flowering in summer. **Conditions:** as
alpina. **Care:** prune in spring; cut back all
previous year's stems almost to their bases.
Propagation: as for *alpina*.

Clematis macropetala
Habit: deciduous climber to about 3.6 m
(12 ft), flowering in spring. **Conditions:** as
alpina. **Care:** can prune after flowering to
restrict size – remove all flowered shoots.
Propagation: as for *alpina*.

Clematis montana 'Rubens'
Habit: vigorous deciduous climber up to 9 m
(30 ft), flowering in spring. **Conditions:** as
alpina. **Care:** prune after flowering to restrict
size; remove all flowered shoots.
Propagation: as for *alpina*.

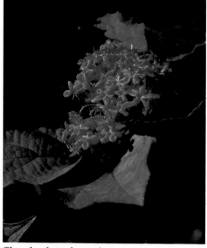

Clematis tangutica
Habit: climber to 6 m (20 ft), flowering in late summer/autumn. **Conditions:** as *alpina*. **Care:** should not need pruning, but to restrict size cut back previous year's stems in spring. **Propagation:** as *alpina*.

Clerodendrum bungei
Habit: deciduous shrub, flowering in late summer; height and spread up to 2.4 m (8 ft). **Conditions:** fertile well-drained soil; full sun and shelter. **Care:** can hard prune in April. **Propagation:** semi-ripe cuttings.

Clethra alnifolia Sweet pepper bush
Habit: deciduous shrub, flowering in summer; height and spread at least 1.8 m (6 ft). **Conditions:** acid, moist, humus-rich soil, sun or partial shade. **Propagation:** semi-ripe cuttings, late summer.

Colutea arborescens Bladder senna
Habit: deciduous shrub, flowering in summer; height and spread 2.4 m (8 ft). **Conditions:** well-drained soil; full sun. **Care:** moderate pruning early spring. **Propagation:** semi-ripe cuttings.

Cornus alba Shrubby dogwood
Habit: deciduous shrub to about 2.4 m (8 ft),
red stems. **Conditions:** thrives in moist/wet
soils, sun or partial shade. **Care:** prune stems
almost to ground level in March.
Propagation: hardwood cuttings.

Cornus alba 'Elegantissima' Shrubby
dogwood
Habit: deciduous shrub grown for its foliage;
2.4 m (8 ft) in height and spread.
Conditions: thrives in moist/wet soils; sun
or partial shade. **Care:** prune stems to within
60 to 90 cm (2 to 3 ft) of the ground in March.

Cornus florida 'Rubra' Flowering dogwood
Habit: deciduous shrub flowering in spring;
height up to 4.5 m (15 ft), spread at least 6 m
(20 ft). **Conditions:** full sun, fertile soil, good
drainage. **Propagation:** simple layering
spring or summer.

Cornus kousa Flowering dogwood
Habit: deciduous shrub flowering in early
summer; height and spread at least 3 m
(10 ft). **Conditions:** full sun, fertile soil, good
drainage. **Propagation:** simple layering in
spring or summer.

Cornus mas   Cornelian cherry
Habit: deciduous shrub, flowering in winter;
with a height and spread of 3.6 m (12 ft).
Conditions: full sun, well-drained fertile soil.
Propagation: the easiest method is simple
layering in spring or summer.

Cornus stolonifera 'Flaviramea'
Shrubby dogwood
Habit: deciduous shrub, yellow stems; height
2.4 m (8 ft). **Conditions:** ideal for moist/wet
soil, full sun or partial shade. **Care:** prune
stems almost to ground level in late winter.
Propagation: hardwood cuttings.

Coronilla emerus
Habit: deciduous shrub flowering in spring;
height and spread about 1.2 m (4 ft).
Conditions: full sun, very good drainage.
Propagation: semi-ripe cuttings can be taken
in August or September.

Corylopsis pauciflora
Habit: a deciduous shrub with scented
flowers in early spring; height and spread
about 1.8 m (6 ft). **Conditions:** sheltered,
sunny spot; well drained, ideally acid soil.
Propagation: simple layering.

Corylus avellana 'Contorta'
Corkscrew hazel
Habit: deciduous shrub with twisted stems; height and spread about 2.4 m (8 ft).
Conditions: any well-drained soil and open position. **Propagation:** simple layering in spring or summer.

Cotinus coggygria   Smoke tree
Habit: deciduous shrub with brilliant autumn leaf colour; height and spread at least 2.4 m (8 ft). **Conditions:** full sun, any well drained soil. **Care:** reduce any straggly shoots in late winter. **Propagation:** layering.

Cotinus coggygria 'Royal Purple'
Purple smoke tree
Habit: deciduous shrub grown for its foliage; height and spread about 2.4 m (8 ft).
Conditions: full sun, any well-drained soil.
Care: can reduce any over-long shoots in late winter. **Propagation:** layering.

Cotoneaster horizontalis
Habit: deciduous shrub, grown for autumn berries; height 60 cm (2 ft), spread up to 2.4 m (8 ft). Can be wall trained to 2.4 m (8 ft) high.
Conditions: any well-drained soil, good on chalk, sunny spot.

Cotoneaster salicifolius
Habit: evergreen shrub with autumn berries; height and spread 3.6 m (12 ft). **Conditions:** as *horizontalis*. **Propagation:** all cotoneasters can be increased from semi-ripe cuttings taken in late summer.

Cryptomeria japonica 'Globosa Nana'
Japanese cedar
Habit: a dwarf evergreen conifer, slow grower, ultimately 2 m (6 ft) high. **Conditions:** best in acid, moist soils, very sunny spot. **Care:** never allow soil to dry out. **Propagation:** semi-ripe cuttings, in summer.

Cytisus decumbens Broom
Habit: prostrate shrub, flowering in early summer; spreading to about 2 m (6 ft). **Conditions:** full sun; best in poor, well-drained soil; tolerates chalk but best in acid soil. **Propagation:** semi-ripe cuttings, summer.

Cytisus × kewensis Broom
Habit: prostrate shrub, height to 60 cm (2 ft), spread 1.2 m (4 ft), spring flowering. **Conditions:** full sun; best in poor, well-drained soil; tolerates chalk but best in acid soil. **Propagation:** semi-ripe cuttings.

Cytisus × *praecox* Broom
Habit: spring-flowering shrub, height and spread 1.8 m (6 ft). **Conditions:** full sun; revels in poor dry soils; best in acid soil but stands chalk. **Propagation:** semi-ripe cuttings, summer.

Cytisus × *praecox* 'Zeelandia' Broom
Habit: one of several varieties. **Conditions and propagation:** as C. × *praecox*. **Care:** after flowering, all brooms should have their seed pods cut off, but do not cut into old wood or it may kill them.

Cytisus scoparius Broom
Habit: spring-flowering shrub with a height and spread of about 2.4 m (8 ft). **Conditions, care and propagation:** as for C. × *praecox*. All cytisus resent root disturbance, so plant young specimens from pots.

Daboecia cantabrica 'Atropurpurea'
St Dabeoc's heath
Habit: dwarf evergreen shrub, flowering in summer; height and spread about 45 cm (18 in). **Conditions:** acid (lime-free), peaty, moist soil; full sun. **Care:** trim off dead flowers. **Propagation:** semi-ripe cuttings.

Danae racemosa Alexandrian laurel
Habit: dwarf evergreen shrub, about 1 by 1 m
(3 by 3 ft), grown mainly for foliage.
Conditions: humus-rich soil, in partial or
complete shade. **Propagation:** established
clumps can be divided in early spring.

Daphne × burkwoodii 'Somerset'
Habit: a semi-evergreen shrub flowering in
late spring; height and spread at least 1.2 m
(4 ft). **Conditions:** any well-drained soil,
including chalk, sun or partial shade.
Propagation: layering in summer.

Daphne cneorum
Habit: a small evergreen, flowering in late
spring; height 15 cm (6 in), spread up to 1 m
(3 ft). A good shrub for rock gardens.
Conditions and propagation: as for
D. × burkwoodii.

Daphne mezereum Mezereon
Habit: popular deciduous late-winter-
flowering shrub, height 1.5 m (5 ft), spread
1.2 m (4 ft). Ideal species for light woodland
conditions. **Conditions and propagation:** as
for *D. × burkwoodii.*

Deutzia × hybrida 'Mont Rose'
Habit: deciduous shrub flowering in early summer; height and spread 1.2 m (4 ft).
Conditions: well-drained soil; full sun or partial shade. **Care:** cut back flowered stems immediately after flowering.
Propagation: semi-ripe cuttings.

Deutzia × lemoinei 'Boule de Neige'
Habit: deciduous shrub about 1 by 1 m (3 by 3 ft), flowering in early summer.
Conditions: any well-drained soil in full sun or partial shade. **Care and propagation:** as 'Mont Rose'.

Elaeagnus pungens 'Maculata'
Habit: evergreen foliage shrub, height and spread approximately 2.4 m (8 ft).
Conditions: well-drained, even poor soils; full sun. **Propagation:** semi-ripe cuttings in early autumn, with undersoil heat.

Enkianthus campanulatus
Habit: deciduous shrub, flowering in spring; height 2.4 m (8 ft), spread 1.5 m (5 ft).
Conditions: acid soil; shelter, dappled shade.
Propagation: layering in spring or summer.

Erica arborea 'Alpina' Tree heath
Habit: evergreen shrub, flowering in spring;
height up to 3.6 m (12 ft), spread 2.4 m (8 ft).
Conditions: acid soil, full sun. **Care:** prune
out any dead wood in spring.
Propagation: semi-ripe cuttings in summer.

Erica ciliaris 'Globosa' Dorset heath
Habit: low-growing evergreen; about 30 by
30 cm (12 by 12 in), summer flowering.
Conditions: needs acid soil and open
position in full sun. **Care:** trim off dead
flowers. **Propagation:** semi-ripe cuttings.

Erica cinerea 'Cevennes' Bell heather
Habit: low evergreen, summer flowering;
height and spread 30 cm (12 in).
Conditions: acid soil and open sunny
position. **Care:** trim off dead flowers.
Propagation: semi-ripe cuttings in summer.

Erica cinerea 'Golden Drop' Bell heather
Habit: grown for its golden foliage; height
and spread 30 cm (12 in). **Conditions:** acid
soil and full sun. **Care:** trim off dead flowers.
Propagation: semi-ripe cuttings in the
summer.

Erica × darleyensis 'Darley Dale' Winter-flowering heather
Habit: winter-flowering evergreen; height about 45 cm (18 in), spread 60 cm (24 in). **Conditions:** will grow in alkaline soils; open sunny position. **Care:** trim off dead flowers. **Propagation:** semi-ripe cuttings.

Erica erigena (E. mediterranea) Tree heath
Habit: evergreen shrub, flowering winter/spring; height 2.4 m (8 ft), spread 1.2 m (4 ft). **Conditions:** will grow on chalky soils; needs sheltered sunny position. Not recommended for very cold areas.

Erica herbacea (E. carnea) 'Myretoun Ruby'
Winter-flowering heather
Habit: low evergreen, height 15 cm (6 in), spread 30 cm (12 in). **Conditions:** grows well in chalky soils; needs open sunny position. **Care:** trim off dead flowers. **Propagation:** semi-ripe cuttings in summer.

Erica tetralix 'Con Underwood'
Cross-leaved heath
Habit: low evergreen, summer flowering; height and spread about 30 cm (12 in). **Conditions:** acid soil and open sunny position. **Care:** trim off dead flowers. **Propagation:** semi-ripe cuttings.

Erica vagans 'St Keverne' Cornish heath
Habit: low-growing evergreen, summer
flowering, height 30 cm (12 in), spread 45 cm
(18 in). **Conditions:** acid soil, open sunny
position. **Care:** trim off dead flowers.
Propagation: semi-ripe cuttings.

Escallonia 'Donard Seedling'
Habit: summer-flowering evergreen shrub;
height and spread about 1.8 m (6 ft).
Conditions: any well-drained soil, full sun.
Care: remove shoots with dead flowers.
Propagation: semi-ripe cuttings.

Euonymus alatus Spindle tree
Habit: deciduous shrub, autumn leaf colour,
height and spread 2.4 m (8 ft).
Conditions: good on chalky soils, ensure
plenty of sun. **Care:** thin out shoots in late
winter if necessary. **Propagation:** semi-ripe
cuttings.

Euonymus europaeus 'Red Cascade'
Spindle tree
Habit: deciduous shrub, autumn berries,
height and spread about 2.4 m (8 ft).
Conditions: good on chalky soils, plenty of
sun. **Care:** if necessary, thin out shoots in late
winter. **Propagation:** semi-ripe cuttings.

Euonymus fortunei 'Emerald Gaiety'
Habit: evergreen foliage shrub, height and spread up to 1.8 m (6 ft). **Conditions:** any soil, sun or partial shade. **Care:** lightly trim if necessary in spring. **Propagation:** semi-ripe cuttings summer/autumn.

Euonymus japonicus 'Aureomarginatus'
Habit: evergreen foliage shrub, height and spread about 2.4 m (8 ft). **Conditions:** any soil, sun or partial shade. **Care:** lightly trim if necessary in spring. **Propagation:** semi-ripe cuttings in summer/autumn.

Exochorda giraldii wilsonii
Habit: deciduous shrub, spring flowering; height and spread 3 m (10 ft). **Conditions:** not recommended for shallow chalk soils; open sunny spot. **Care:** cut out oldest wood after flowering. **Propagation:** soft cuttings.

Forsythia × intermedia
Habit: deciduous spring-flowering shrub; height and spread at least 2.4 m (8 ft). **Conditions:** any soil, sun or partial shade. **Care:** prune back flowered shoots after flowering. **Propagation:** hardwood cuttings.

Fothergilla major
Habit: deciduous shrub, spring flowering; height and spread at least 2.4 m (8 ft). **Conditions:** acid, moist, peaty soil, sun or partial shade. **Propagation:** simple layering in spring or summer.

Fuchsia magellanica 'Gracilis'
Habit: deciduous shrub, summer flowering; height and spread 90 cm (3 ft). **Conditions:** well-drained soil, full sun or partial shade. **Care:** prune to ground in late winter. **Propagation:** softwood cuttings.

Gaultheria procumbens   Partridge berry
Habit: evergreen shrub, autumn berries; height 15 cm (6 in), spread 90 cm (3 ft). **Conditions:** acid, moist, peaty soil, in partial shade. **Propagation:** semi-ripe cuttings in summer.

Genista lydia   Broom
Habit: a dwarf shrub, spring flowering; height 60 cm (24 in), spread 1.8 m (6 ft). **Conditions:** well- drained soil, full sun. Ideal for dry banks. **Propagation:** semi-ripe cuttings in late summer.

Halesia carolina Snowdrop tree
Habit: deciduous shrub, spring flowering;
height 6 m (20 ft), spread 7.6 m (25 ft).
Conditions: acid, moist, peaty soil, sun or
dappled shade. **Propagation:** simple layering
in spring or summer.

Hamamelis mollis Chinese witch hazel
Habit: deciduous shrub, winter flowering;
height and spread 3.6 m (12 ft).
Conditions: acid or neutral, moist, peaty soil;
dappled shade. **Propagation:** simple layering
in spring or summer.

Hebe × andersonii Shrubby veronica
Habit: evergreen shrub, summer flowering;
height and spread 90 cm (3 ft).
Conditions: any well-drained soil, full sun,
sheltered spot. **Care:** trim off dead flowers.
Propagation: semi-ripe cuttings, late
summer.

Hebe armstrongii Shrubby veronica
Habit: evergreen shrub for foliage; height
and spread 90 cm (3 ft). **Conditions:** any well-
drained soil, full sun, sheltered spot.
Care: trim off dead flowers.
Propagation: semi-ripe cuttings, late
summer.

Hedera colchica 'Dentata Variegata'
Variegated Persian ivy
Habit: evergreen climber for foliage; height
up to 9 m (30 ft). Can also be used as ground
cover. **Conditions:** any soil, sun or shade.
Care: trim hard in April if necessary.
Propagation: soft cuttings, late spring.

Hedera helix 'Sagittaefolia' Variety of
common ivy
Habit: evergreen climber, can also be used as
ground cover. **Conditions:** any soil, sun or
shade. **Care:** trim hard in April if necessary.
Propagation: soft cuttings taken in late
spring.

Helianthemum nummularium variety
Rock rose
Habit: creeping evergreen shrub, summer
flowering; height 15 cm (6 in), spread 60 cm
(24 in). **Conditions:** well-drained, even poor
soil, full sun. **Propagation:** semi-ripe
cuttings.

Hibiscus syriacus 'Coeleste'
Habit: deciduous shrub, summer/autumn
flowering; height and spread 1.8 m (6 ft).
Conditions: well-drained soil,
full sun. Sheltered spot in very cold areas.
Propagation: semi-ripe cuttings/layering.

Hippophae rhamnoides Sea buckthorn
Habit: deciduous shrub, autumn/winter
berries; height and spread at least 2.4 m (8 ft).
Conditions: any well-drained soil, sun, ideal
for seaside gardens. **Propagation:** seeds sown
in spring.

Holodiscus discolor
Habit: deciduous shrub, flowering in
summer; height and spread about 2.4 m (8 ft).
Conditions: moist but well-drained soil, full
sun. **Propagation:** semi-ripe or hardwood
cuttings.

Hydrangea petiolaris Climbing hydrangea
Habit: deciduous climber, summer
flowering; height at least 7.6 m (25 ft), spread
4.5 m (15 ft). **Conditions:** moist soil in sun or
shade. **Propagation:** serpentine layering in
spring or summer.

Hydrangea macrophylla Common
hydrangea
Habit: deciduous summer-flowering shrub;
height and spread at least 1.8 m (6 ft).
Conditions: moist soil in sun or shade.
Care: cut out oldest stems in late winter,
remove dead flowers. **Propagation:** cuttings.

Hydrangea paniculata 'Grandiflora'
Habit: deciduous shrub, flowering late
summer; height and spread at least 3.6 m
(12 ft). **Conditions:** moist soil in sun or shade.
Care: all stems can be cut back hard in early
spring. **Propagation:** cuttings.

Hypericum calycinum   Rose of Sharon
Habit: ground-cover evergreen, summer
flowering; height 30 cm (12 in).
Conditions: grows anywhere; sun or shade.
Care: cut almost to ground every two years
in March. **Propagation:** division in winter.

Ilex × altaclarensis 'Golden King'   Holly
Habit: evergreen shrub for foliage; height at
least 6 m (20 ft), spread up to 4.5 m (15 ft).
Conditions: any ordinary soil, preferably
moist; full sun for best colour. **Care:** can be
pruned in April. **Propagation:** semi-ripe
cuttings.

Ilex aquifolium 'J.C. van Tol'   Holly
Habit: evergreen shrub for berries; height at
least 4.5 m (15 ft), spread 3 m (10 ft).
Conditions: Any ordinary soil, preferably
moist; sun or shade. **Care:** can be pruned in
April. **Propagation:** semi-ripe cuttings.

Ilex crenata 'Golden Gem' Holly
Habit: dwarf foliage shrub; height up to
60 cm (24 in), spread to 90 cm (3 ft).
Conditions: any ordinary soil, preferably
moist; full sun for best colour. **Care:** can be
pruned in April. **Propagation:** semi-ripe
cuttings.

Jasminum nudiflorum Winter jasmine
Habit: deciduous climber flowering in
winter; height about 3 m (10 ft).
Conditions: ordinary well-drained soil; sun
or shade. **Care:** cut back flowered shoots after
flowering, to 5 cm (2 in).
Propagation: hardwood cuttings.

Juniperus chinensis 'Hetzii' Chinese
juniper
Habit: evergreen, spreading ground-cover
conifer. **Conditions:** well-drained soil,
including chalk; shade or full sun. **Care:** can
be trimmed to shape if necessary in April.
Propagation: semi-ripe cuttings.

Juniperus chinensis 'Pfitzerana Aurea'
Chinese juniper
Habit: evergreen, spreading ground-cover
conifer; height 90 cm (3 ft), spread 1.5 m (5 ft).
Conditions: well-drained soil, including
chalk; full sun for best colour. **Care:** trim in
April. **Propagation:** semi-ripe cuttings.

Juniperus communis 'Compressa'
Variety of common juniper
Habit: evergreen, ideal for rock gardens; height about 60 cm (24 in), but slow growing. **Conditions:** well-drained soil, including chalk; full sun or partial shade.
Propagation: semi-ripe cuttings.

Juniperus conferta   Shore juniper
Habit: evergreen ground-cover conifer; height up to 45 cm (18 in), spread about 4 m (13 ft). **Conditions:** well-drained soil, including chalk; sun or partial shade.
Care: can be trimmed in April.
Propagation: semi-ripe cuttings.

Juniperus virginiana 'Skyrocket'
Habit: evergreen, very narrow habit; height 6 m (20 ft). **Conditions:** well-drained soil, including chalk; sun or partial shade.
Propagation: semi-ripe cuttings in autumn.

Kalmia latifolia   Calico bush
Habit: evergreen shrub, flowering in early summer; height and spread 2.4 m (8 ft) plus. **Conditions:** acid, moist, peaty soil, partial or dappled shade. **Care:** remove dead flowers. **Propagation:** layering.

Kerria japonica 'Pleniflora' Jew's mallow
Habit: deciduous shrub, flowering in spring;
height up to 3.6 m (12 ft), spread about 1.2 m
(4 ft). **Conditions:** ordinary soil, sun or partial
shade. **Care:** after flowering cut out all
flowered stems. **Propagation:** hardwood
cuttings.

Kolkwitzia amabilis Beauty bush
Habit: deciduous shrub, flowering in early
summer; height up to 3.6 m (12 ft), spread up
to 2.4 m (8 ft). **Conditions:** ordinary soil, full
sun. **Care:** prune after flowering; remove the
oldest stems. **Propagation:** semi-ripe cuttings
with heat.

Lavandula angustifolia Old English
lavender
Habit: evergreen shrub, summer flowering;
height and spread up to 1.2 m (4 ft).
Conditions: good drainage, full sun.
Care: trim off dead flowers.
Propagation: semi-ripe cuttings, summer.

Leycesteria formosa
Habit: deciduous shrub, flowering in late
summer; height and spread about 1.8 m (6 ft).
Conditions: shade or full sun, and good
drainage. **Care:** remove all the old flowered
stems in early March. **Propagation:** seed.

Lonicera japonica 'Aureoreticulata'
Japanese honeysuckle
Habit: evergreen climber to 7.6 m (25 ft),
grown for its foliage. **Conditions:** humus-
rich, well-drained soil; sun or partial shade.
Care: can be thinned out in late winter.
Propagation: semi-ripe cuttings.

Lonicera periclymenum 'Belgica'   Early
Dutch honeysuckle
Habit: deciduous climber flowering in early
summer; height up to 6 m (20 ft).
Conditions: humus-rich, well-drained soil;
sun or partial shade. **Care:** can be thinned
out in late winter. **Propagation:** cuttings.

Magnolia × soulangiana 'Lennei'
Habit: deciduous shrub flowering in spring;
height and spread up to 4.5 m (15 ft).
Conditions: rich loamy soil best; shelter from
cold winds; full sun or partial shade.
Propagation: layering, spring/summer.

Mahonia aquifolium   Oregon grape
Habit: evergreen shrub, flowering in early
spring; height and spread up to 1.5 m (5 ft).
Conditions: grows in any soil, sun or partial
shade. **Care:** can, if desired, be pruned hard
back in April. **Propagation:** semi-ripe
cuttings.

Mahonia bealei
Habit: evergreen shrub, flowering in winter; height and spread around 2.4 m (8 ft). **Conditions:** fertile, well-drained soil, sun or partial shade. **Propagation:** semi-ripe cuttings in autumn.

× *Osmarea burkwoodii*
Habit: evergreen shrub, fragrant flowers in spring; height and spread at least 1.8 m (6 ft). **Conditions:** any soil suitable; full sun or partial shade. **Propagation:** semi-ripe cuttings in autumn.

Pachysandra terminalis
Habit: evergreen ground-cover plant; height 30 cm (12 in), spread 45 cm (18 in). **Conditions:** any soil, partial or heavy shade. **Propagation:** plants can be lifted and divided into smaller pieces in March.

Parrotia persica
Habit: deciduous shrub, grown for its autumn leaf colour; height at least 6 m (20 ft), spread at least 4.5 m (15 ft). **Conditions:** good drainage, fertile loamy soil; sun or partial shade.

Parthenocissus henryana Chinese Virginia creeper
Habit: vigorous deciduous climber for autumn leaf colour; self-clinging; height up to 9 m (30 ft). **Conditions:** shelter, light shade or sun; any soil. **Care:** can be pruned back in summer.

Pernettya mucronata
Habit: low-growing ground-cover shrub, evergreen, autumn fruits; height and spread up to 90 cm (3 ft). **Conditions:** plant male and female plants; acid, moist, peaty soil; sun or partial shade.

Philadelphus hybrid 'Belle Etoile'
Mock orange
Habit: deciduous shrub, fragrant flowers early summer; height and spread 3 m (10 ft).
Conditions: any well-drained soil, good on chalk; full sun. **Care:** cut back flowered stems after flowering. **Propagation:** cuttings.

Pieris formosa 'Forrestii'
Habit: evergreen shrub, red young foliage, white flowers in spring; height and spread at least 3.6 m (12 ft). **Conditions:** acid, moist, peaty soil, partial shade, shelter.
Care: remove dead flowers.

Poncirus trifoliata   Japanese bitter orange
Habit: spiny shrub producing scented flowers in spring; height and spread 3 m (10 ft). **Conditions:** any fertile soil in sun. **Propagation:** semi-ripe cuttings in late summer.

Potentilla fruticosa   Shrubby cinquefoil
Habit: small deciduous shrub flowering summer and autumn; average height 90 cm (3 ft), similar spread, varies with variety. **Conditions:** well-drained soil, full sun. **Care:** trim off dead flowers.

Pyracantha coccinea   Firethorn
Habit: evergreen shrub grown for autumn berries; height and spread at least 3.6 m (12 ft). **Conditions:** any well-drained soil, good on chalk; partial shade or full sun. **Propagation:** semi-ripe cuttings.

Rhododendron 'Blue Tit'
Habit: evergreen shrub, spring flowering; height and spread about 90 cm (3 ft). **Conditions:** acid, moist, peaty soil, partial shade. **Care:** remove dead flowers. **Propagation:** simple layering.

Rhododendron 'Hardijzer Beauty'
An evergreen azalea
Habit: evergreen shrub, flowering late
spring; height and spread 90 cm (3 ft).
Conditions: acid, moist, peaty soil, partial
shade. **Care:** remove dead flowers.
Propagation: simple layering.

Rhodendron 'Klondyke' A deciduous
azalea
Habit: deciduous shrub, flowering late
spring/early summer; height and spread
1.8 m (6 ft). **Conditions:** acid, moist, peaty
soil; partial shade. **Care:** remove dead
flowers. **Propagation:** simple layering.

Rhododendron × praecox Winter-
flowering rhododendron
Habit: evergreen shrub, winter flowering;
height and spread around 1.2 m (4 ft).
Conditions: acid, moist, peaty soil, partial
shade. **Care:** remove dead flowers.
Propagation: simple layering, spring/summer.

Rhododendron 'Elizabeth Hobbie'
Habit: evergreen shrub, flowering late
spring; height and spread about 60 cm
(24 in). **Conditions:** acid, moist, peaty soil,
partial shade. **Care:** remove dead flowers.
Propagation: simple layering.

Rhododendron 'Furnival's Daughter'
Habit: evergreen shrub, flowering late spring; height and spread about 3.6 m (12 ft). **Conditions:** acid, moist, peaty soil, partial shade. **Care:** remove dead flowers. **Propagation:** simple layering.

Rhododendron 'Koster's Cream'
Habit: evergreen shrub, flowering late spring; height and spread about 1.8 m (6 ft). **Conditions:** acid, moist, peaty soil, partial shade. **Care:** remove dead flowers. **Propagation:** simple layering.

Rhododendron 'Louis Pasteur'
Habit: evergreen shrub, flowering late spring; height and spread at least 3.6 m (12 ft). **Conditions:** acid, moist, peaty soil, partial shade. **Care:** remove dead flowers. **Propagation:** simple layering.

Rhus typhina 'Laciniata'   Stag's horn sumach
Habit: deciduous shrub for autumn leaf colour; height and spread at least 3.6 m (12 ft). **Conditions:** any soil, sunny spot. **Care:** can be pruned back hard in late winter. **Propagation:** rooted suckers.

Ribes sanguineum 'Carneum'   Flowering currant
Habit: deciduous shrub, flowering in spring; height and spread about 1.8 m (6 ft).
Conditions: any well-drained soil, sun or partial shade. **Care:** remove old wood after flowering. **Propagation:** hardwood cuttings.

Rosa moyesii 'Geranium'   Shrub rose
Habit: deciduous shrub, red flowers, autumn hips; height and spread around 2.4 m (8 ft).
Conditions: fertile soil, full sun. **Care:** feed well in spring and summer; prune out very old wood in March.

Rosa rubiginosa   Sweet briar
Habit: deciduous shrub rose, flowering in early summer; autumn hips; height and spread about 2.4 m (8 ft). **Conditions:** fertile soil, full sun. **Care:** feed well in spring and summer; prune out very old wood in March.

Rosa villosa (R. pomifera)   Apple rose
Habit: deciduous shrub, pale pink flowers early summer, autumn hips; height and spread about 1.8 m (6 ft). **Conditions:** fertile soil, full sun. **Care:** feed well in spring and summer; prune out very old wood in March.

Rubus thibetanus Ornamental bramble
Habit: deciduous shrub grown for winter
stem colour; height and spread 1.8 to 2.4 m (6
to 8 ft). **Conditions:** well-drained soil, sun or
partial shade. **Care:** cut down stems to near
ground in March.

Sambucus racemosa 'Plumosa Aurea'
Golden red-berried elder
Habit: deciduous shrub, grown for its
foliage; height and spread about 2.4 m (8 ft).
Conditions: any fertile soil, sun or partial
shade. **Care:** can hard prune in March for
better foliage colour.

Santolina chamaecyparissus Cotton
lavender
Habit: evergreen shrub for foliage effect;
flowering July; height and spread about
60 cm (24 in). **Conditions:** good drainage, full
sun. **Care:** cut off dead flowers.
Propagation: semi-ripe cuttings, summer.

Sarcococca humilis Christmas Box
Habit: evergreen shrub, white fragrant
flowers late winter; height and spread about
45 cm (18 in). **Conditions:** fertile soil,
including chalk, partial shade.
Propagation: division in spring.

Skimmia japonica
Habit: evergreen shrub, white flowers in spring, red berries; plant male and female plants together for berry production; height and spread about 1.5 m (5 ft).
Conditions: ordinary soil, sun or partial shade.

Solanum crispum Chilean potato tree
Habit: vigorous semi-evergreen climber, flowering in summer; height up to 6 m (20 ft).
Conditions: any soil, against south or west wall. **Care:** previous year's shoots pruned hard back in April.

Spartium junceum Spanish broom
Habit: deciduous shrub, flowering in summer; height 3.6 m (12 ft), spread 2.4 m (8 ft). **Conditions:** very well-drained soil, full sun. **Care:** cut off dead flowers.
Propagation: seeds in spring.

Spiraea × arguta Foam of May
Habit: deciduous shrub, flowering in spring; height and spread 1.8 m (6 ft).
Conditions: needs fertile soil and full sun.
Care: cut back flowered stems after flowering. **Propagation:** soft cuttings.

Spiraea × bumalda 'Anthony Waterer'
Habit: deciduous shrub, flowering late summer; height and spread about 60 cm (24 in). **Conditions:** needs fertile soil and full sun. **Care:** prune hard back in March. **Propagation:** soft cuttings in spring.

Stachyurus praecox
Habit: deciduous shrub, flowering from late winter to spring; height and spread at least 2.4 m (8 ft). **Conditions:** ordinary soil, with plenty of peat added; sun or partial shade. **Propagation:** layering.

Stranvaesia davidiana
Habit: evergreen shrub, grown for its autumn berries; height and spread up to 6 m (20 ft). **Conditions:** any well-drained, fertile soil, sun or partial shade. **Propagation:** simple layering.

Symphoricarpos albus 'Laevigatus'
Snowberry
Habit: deciduous shrub, grown for its berries; height and spread about 1.8 m (6 ft). **Conditions:** grows anywhere, shade or sun. **Care:** if necessary, thin out stems in winter. **Propagation:** hardwood cuttings.

Syringa* × *persica Persian lilac
Habit: deciduous shrub, fragrant flowers late spring; height and spread 1.8 m (6 ft) plus.
Conditions: any fertile soil, sun or partial shade. **Care:** cut off dead flowers.
Propagation: semi-ripe cuttings.

Syringa vulgaris variety Common lilac
Habit: deciduous shrub, flowering in late spring; many varieties and colours; height up to 3.6 m (12 ft), spread 3 m (10 ft).
Conditions: any fertile soil, sun or partial shade. **Care:** cut off dead flowers.

Taxus baccata 'Dovastonii Aurea' Yew
Habit: evergreen conifer for foliage effect; height and spread up to 4 m (14 ft).
Conditions: any soil type, good on chalk; full sun for best colour. **Propagation:** semi-ripe cuttings.

Taxus baccata 'Fastigiata Aurea' Golden Irish yew
Habit: evergreen conifer for foliage effect; slim habit to height of 5 m (16 ft).
Conditions: any soil type, good on chalk; full sun for best colour. **Propagation:** semi-ripe cuttings.

Viburnum × burkwoodii
Habit: evergreen shrub, scented flowers in spring; height and spread at least 2.4 m (8 ft). **Conditions:** fertile, moist soils, good on chalk; full sun. **Care:** thin out old wood after flowering.

Viburnum davidii
Habit: dwarf evergreen shrub, grown mainly for its foliage; flowers in early summer; height and spread around 90 cm (3 ft). **Conditions:** fertile moist soils, good on chalk. **Propagation:** semi-ripe cuttings.

Viburnum farreri (V. fragrans)
Habit: deciduous shrub, flowering in winter; height and spread around 2.4 m (8 ft). **Conditions:** fertile moist soils, good on chalk; full sun. **Care:** prune out old wood after flowering.

Viburnum opulus 'Notcutt's Variety'
Guelder rose
Habit: deciduous shrub grown for its autumn berries; height and spread at least 3.6 m (12 ft). **Conditions:** fertile moist soils, good on chalk; full sun. **Care:** prune out old wood in winter.

Viburnum plicatum tomentosum Japanese
snowball
Habit: deciduous shrub, flowering in late
spring; height and spread 3 m (10 ft).
Conditions: moist fertile soil, good on chalk;
full sun. **Care:** prune out old wood after
flowering.

Viburnum tinus Laurustinus
Habit: evergreen shrub, flowering in winter
and spring; height and spread at least 2.4 m
(8 ft). **Conditions:** moist fertile soil, good on
chalk; full sun or partial shade. **Care:** prune
out old wood after flowering.

Vinca minor 'Atropurpurea' Lesser
periwinkle
Habit: ground-cover evergreen, flowering in
spring and summer; spreads to about 90 cm
(3 ft). **Conditions:** any well-drained soil;
partial shade. **Propagation:** easily increased
by division in winter.

Vitis coignetiae Japanese crimson glory
vine
Habit: vigorous climber grown for autumn
leaf colour; can grow up to 27 m (90 ft) in
height. **Conditions:** deep, rich, moist soil,
best on south or west wall. **Care:** can prune
back in late summer if too large.

Vitis 'Brant' Grape vine
Habit: deciduous climber, edible fruits, autumn leaf colour; height at least 6 m (20 ft). **Conditions:** deep, rich, moist soil; full sun. **Care:** prune back all side shoots in winter, to within one bud.

Weigela hybrid
Habit: deciduous shrub, flowering early summer; several varieties and colours; height and spread 1.5 to 1.8 m (5 to 6 ft). **Conditions:** fertile, moist, well-drained soil; sun or partial shade. **Care:** after flowering, cut back old flowered stems.

Wisteria sinensis Chinese wisteria
Habit: deciduous climber flowering in spring; height to 30 m (100 ft). **Conditions:** fertile, moist soil; south- or west-facing wall. **Care:** in late winter reduce all previous year's side growths to two buds.

Yucca flaccida
Habit: dwarf evergreen; summer flowering; 1.2 m (4 ft) high flower stem. **Conditions:** dry, well-drained soil, full sun. Can be grown successfully even in poor stony soils. **Care:** cut off old stem after flowering.

PLANTS FOR SPECIAL PURPOSES

Permanent shade

Aucuba
Danae
Hedera
Hydrangea
Hypericum
Ilex
Jasminum
Juniperus
Pachysandra
Parthenocissus
Symphoricarpos

Hot dry positions

Colutea
Coronilla
Cytisus
Genista
Helianthemum
Juniperus
Lavandula
Potentilla
Santolina
Spartium
Yucca

Very chalky soils

Berberis
Buddleia
Ceanothus
Clematis
Corylus
Cotoneaster
Daphne × burkwoodii
Erica × darleyensis
Erica erigena
Erica herbacea
Euonymus
Juniperus
Lonicera
Philadelphus
Pyracantha
Sarcococca
Taxus
Viburnum

Wet soils

Cornus alba
Cornus stolonifera
  'Flaviramea'
Sambucus
Symphoricarpos

Autumn leaf colour/berries

Acer
Berberis thunbergii
Berberis wilsoniae
Celastrus
Cotinus coggygria
Cotoneaster
Euonymus alatus
Euonymus europaeus
Gaultheria
Hippophae
Ilex aquifolium 'J.C.
  van Tol'
Parrotia
Parthenocissus
Pernettya
Pyracantha
Rhus
Rosa
Skimmia
Stranvaesia
Symphoricarpos
Viburnum opulus
Vitis

continued overleaf

Coloured-foliage shrubs

Actinidia
Aucuba
Calluna vulgaris 'Gold Haze'
Chamaecyparis
Cornus alba 'Elegantissima'
Cotinus coggygria 'Royal Purple'
Elaeagnus pungens 'Maculata'
Erica cinerea 'Golden Drop'
Euonymus fortunei 'Emerald Gaiety'
Euonymus japonicus 'Aureomarginatus'
Hebe armstrongii
Hedera colchica 'Dentata Variegata'
Ilex × altaclarensis 'Golden King'
Ilex crenata 'Golden Gem'
Juniperus
Lavandula
Lonicera japonica 'Aureoreticulata'
Pieris formosa 'Forrestii'
Sambucus racemosa 'Plumosa Aurea'
Santolina
Taxus

Winter stem colour

Cornus alba
Cornus stolonifera 'Flaviramea'
Leycesteria
Rubus

Winter flower colour

Cornus mas
Daphne mezereum
Erica × darleyensis
Erica erigena
Erica herbacea
Hamamelis
Jasminum nudiflorum
Mahonia bealei
Rhododendron × praecox
Sarcococca
Stachyurus
Viburnum farreri
Viburnum tinus

COMMON NAME INDEX